Fog and Mist

Elizabeth Miles

Heinemann Library
Chicago, Illinois

Designed by Richard Parker and Q2A Solutions
Illustrations: Jeff Edwards
Originated by Dot Gradations Ltd.
Printed and bound in China by South China Printing Company

12
10 9 8 7 6 5 4

Library of Congress Cataloging-in-Publication Data
Miles, Elizabeth, 1960-
    Fog and mist / Elizabeth Miles.
        p. cm. -- (Watching the weather)
    Includes bibliographical references and index.
    ISBN 1-4034-6552-5 -- ISBN 1-4034-6557-6 (pbk.)
    ISBN 978-1-4034-6552-8 -- ISBN 978-1-4034-6557-3 (pbk.)
1. Fog--Juvenile literature. 2. Water vapor, Atmospheric--Juvenile literature. I. Title. II. Series.
    QC929.F7M55 2005
    551.57'5--dc22
                        2004018491

Acknowledgments
The Publishers would like to thank the following for permission to reproduce photographs: Alamy pp. 17 (Justin Kase), 18 (Dennis Hallinan), 25 (K-PHOTOS); Corbis pp. 5 (Tim Thompson), 6 (Owen Franken), 8 (Dick Durrance II), 9 (Dick Durrance II), 11 (Craig Tuttle), 12 (Owen Franken), 16, 26 (Nik Wheeler); Getty Images pp. 7 (Photographer's Choice/Jonathan Gale), 13 (Image Bank/Joseph Devenney), 15 (PhotoDisc); Network pp. 22 (Jean-Claude Coutausse), 23 (Jean-Claude Coutausse); NHPA pp. 20 (Nigel J Dennis), 21 (Anthony Bannister); PA Photos p. 4(EPA); Rex Features p. 14 (Shout); Science Photo Library pp. 24 (Dr Juerg Alean), 27 (Mark Clarke); The Weather Channel p. 16; Tudor Photography pp. 28, 29.

Cover photograph of mist surrounding Jinshanling, Great Wall of China, reproduced with permission of Getty Images/Digital Vision.

The Publishers would like to thank Daniel Ogden for his assistance in the preparation of this book.

Every effort has been made to contact copyright holders of any material reproduced in this book. Any omissions will be rectified in subsequent printings if notice is given to the Publisher.

Contents

Some words are shown in bold, **like this**. You can find out what they mean by looking in the glossary.

What Are Fog and Mist?

Fog and mist are clouds that are on or near the ground. They make everything look **hazy**. Fog can be dangerous because it is difficult to see through.

In fog, drivers may turn on their headlights. This helps them to see the road ahead more easily.

Mist is easier to see through than fog.

In thick fog, you might not be able to see the other side of a road. Mist is thinner. It is easier to see through.

What Are Fog and Mist Made Of?

Fog and mist are made of lots of tiny water **droplets**. The droplets float in the air near the ground.

The water droplets in fog can make it difficult to see even very large objects.

The water droplets in mist are farther apart. That is why it is easier to see through mist.

Even a small amount of fog or mist is made up of hundreds of water droplets. Fog feels wetter than mist because foggy air has more water droplets.

Is It Foggy or Misty?

It is foggy when you cannot clearly see anything more than a couple of miles away.

Sometimes fog is so thick that you cannot see very far ahead.

Mist is less dangerous than fog because you can see through it more easily.

It is misty when you can clearly see everything close by. Things look **hazy** in the distance when it is misty.

How Do Fog and Mist Form?

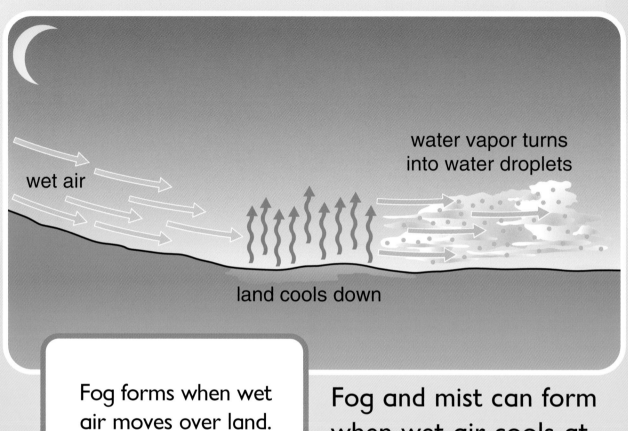

wet air

water vapor turns into water droplets

land cools down

Fog forms when wet air moves over land.

Fog and mist can form when wet air cools at night. At night, the ground often cools down the air close to it. This turns **water vapor** into water **droplets**.

When the water droplets turn back into water vapor, the mist clears.

In the morning, the sun warms the ground. This heats the air near the ground and clears the mist and fog.

Fog at sea

Fog often forms at sea. This can happen when warm, moist air passes over cold water.

Fog often fills San Francisco Bay, on the west coast of the United States.

Some ships sound **foghorns** so that other ships can hear them coming.

Fog at sea can be dangerous for ships. If they cannot see ahead, they might sail into rocks or other ships. Ships can use **radar** to find their way in the fog.

High and Low Fog

Fog can form on high ground where the air is cold. Mountaineers and walkers can get lost in the fog.

If thick fog forms, hikers cannot see the path ahead.

Fog often forms near the low ground in **valleys**. This is because cool, wet air sinks below warm air and settles in the valley.

Cool, wet air in a valley can turn into thick fog.

Fog Warnings

Fog can be dangerous. It is important to warn people if it might form. Car drivers may choose to stay at home if it is going to be foggy.

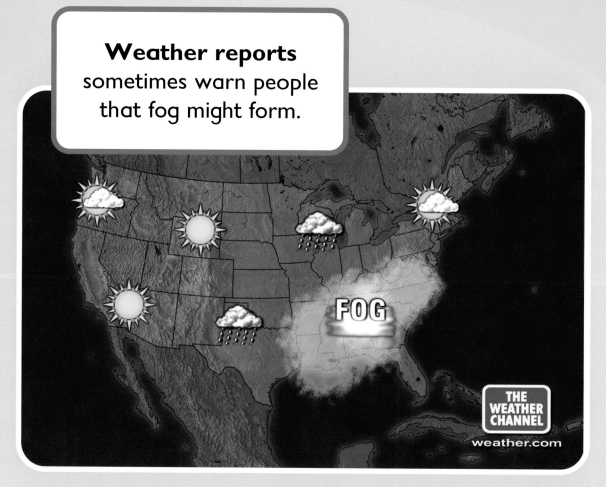

Weather reports sometimes warn people that fog might form.

If fog is **forecast**, signs are switched on next to the road. They stay on until the fog clears.

Road signs warn drivers to slow down because there is fog ahead.

Fog Lights and Sounds

Driving in fog is dangerous because it is hard to see the cars in front. Drivers turn on their headlights and fog lights to see better.

Drivers need to go very slowly in heavy fog.

Lighthouse beams are very bright. You can see them through thick fog.

In foggy weather, at night, and in storms, lighthouses warn ships that land is near. They shine a beam of light and sound a **foghorn**.

Mist, Plants, and Animals

Plants and animals need water to live. Sometimes in hot, dry deserts, water **droplets** from mist are the only water available.

Some desert plants have wide, long leaves that take in water droplets left by the morning mist.

Water runs down this beetle's back and into its mouth.

Some desert beetles collect water to drink from the early morning mist. They stand in the mist while water droplets form on their backs.

Mist, Fog, and People

In some dry desert areas, people do not have enough water to drink. For extra water, some villages collect water from the mist or fog.

The water **droplets** from mist collect on nets and drip down into containers below.

The mist that collects on these nets is a way of getting extra water in the desert.

Water from the mist or fog is cleaned and then stored. Villagers can use the water for drinking or cooking when there is little rain.

Disaster: Freezing Fog

Rime is made of ice and can get very thick.

Freezing fog forms when water **droplets** in the air get very cold. The droplets are so cold that they turn into **rime** as soon as they touch a cold surface.

Passenger jets fly very high through clouds where the air can be very cold. Rime can gather on airplane wings and affect the controls.

Special equipment on high-flying airplanes melts the ice that can gather.

Is It Fog?

In towns and cities, **haze** that looks like fog might be smog. In smog, each water **droplet** forms on a speck of dirt in the air.

Smog is a mix of fog and smoke, or pollution.

Smog can harm our health and the **environment**. Some people try to make less **pollution**. Driving a car causes pollution, so some people use a bicycle instead.

Sometimes people wear masks so that they breathe in less smog.

Project: Making Mist

Now that you know that mist and fog are made from water **droplets**, try making your own mist at home.

You will need:
- six or more ice cubes
- a metal plate or dish
- warm water
- a large glass or jar

1. Place the ice on the metal plate and put it in a fridge until the plate is very cold.

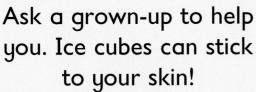

Ask a grown-up to help you. Ice cubes can stick to your skin!

2. Pour warm water—about as deep as your thumb—into the bottom of the glass.

3. Quickly place the ice-cold plate on top of the glass, while the water is still warm.

4. Mist will form inside the glass.

Glossary

droplet very small drop of water

environment world around us and all the living things in it

foghorn warning horn used by ships and lighthouses

forecast try to figure out what the weather will be in the future

haze a thin mist that makes things in the distance look slightly unclear

pollution smoke or dirt that can damage the environment. Pollution can come from cars and factories.

radar equipment that uses radio waves to see objects ahead

rime kind of frost

valley low area of land surrounded by hills

water vapor water in the air. Water vapor is a gas that we cannot see.

weather report information that says what the weather is going to be

More Books to Read

Ganeri, Anita. *Nature's Patterns: Seasons*. Chicago: Heinemann Library, 2004.

Hughes, Monica. *Nature's Patterns: Weather Patterns*. Chicago: Heinemann Library, 2004.

Hughes, Monica. *Seasons: Winter*. Chicago: Raintree, 2003.

Index